THE BELLFOUNTAIN GIANT KILLERS

The Story of a Small Oregon High School
and its Miraculous Championship Season

Joe R. Blakely

Bear Creek Press

Also by Joe R. Blakely

THE TALL FIRS

THE STORY OF THE UNIVERSITY OF OREGON &
THE FIRST NCAA BASKETBALL CHAMPIONSHIP

Bellfountain school and gymnasium, 1937
the year the Bellfountain "Giant Killers" won the Oregon state basketball championship

THE BELLFOUNTAIN GIANT KILLERS
by Joe R. Blakely

Copyright © 2003 by Joe R. Blakely
www.bearcreekpress.com/joe_blakely.html

HISTORICAL PHOTOGRAPHS PROVIDED BY
Alvah Hinton, Richard Litchfield, and Harry and Treva Wallace

CONTEMPORARY PHOTOGRAPHS BY
Joe R. Blakely

HISTORICAL MATERIALS OR RESEARCH ASSISTANCE PROVIDED BY
Benton County Historical Museum and Willamette University

PUBLISHED BY
Bear Creek Press
814 Couch Avenue • Wallowa, Oregon 97885
541-886-9020 • bearcreekpress@eoni.com
www.bearcreekpress.com

PRINTING HISTORY
Bear Creek Press First Edition, January 2003

Printed in the United States of America.

ISBN: 1-930111-24-X

Front cover photograph:
Four starters on the Bellfountain "Giant Killers" 1937 state championship basketball team.
From left: Stanley Buckingham, Harry Wallace, Richard Kessler, Clifford Larkin.
Not pictured: Frank Buckingham

World Headquarters located in Wallowa, Oregon U.S.A.
(at the old Abbie Riggle place on Bear Creek Road).

Acknowledgments

The writing of this book could not have been accomplished without the help of many people. To these people I wish to dedicate this book:

To Saundra Miles for her constant support.

To the people I interviewed who tried so hard to remember—Alvah Hinton, Clifford Larkin, Wayne Giesy, and Harold Hendrix.

A special thanks to Richard and Ralph Litchfield.

Most of all I'd like to thank Harry and Treva Wallace. One day they found me on their front porch, and four hours later I emerged out their front door with a full belly, a handful of photographs and, of course, their experiences while growing up in Bellfountain.

Lastly, I'd like to thank Mark Highberger for his steadfast belief in the resurrection of this sensational story.

–Joe. R. Blakely

Bellfountain, Oregon: "that wide place in the road"
–*The Oregon Statesman*, March 23, 1937

Contents

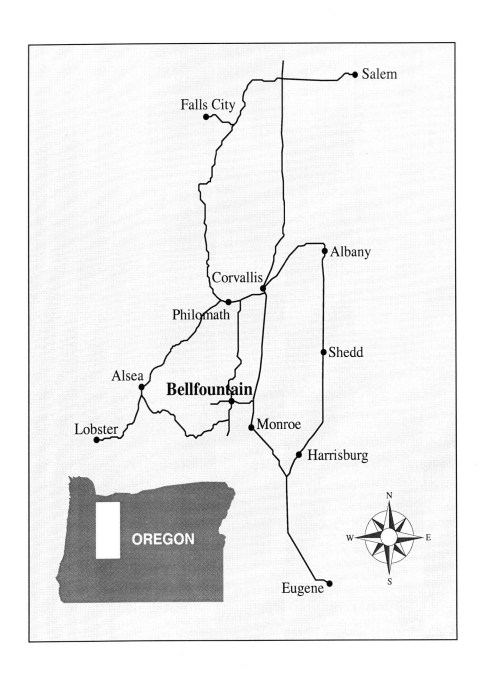

The Semi-Final Game

This was the game that 3,000 screaming fans had waited for. They crammed the balconies and spilled out onto the court at Willamette University in Salem, Oregon, where the semi-final game of the 1937 Oregon State High School Basketball Tournament was about to begin.

The game pitted Bellfountain High School, located at a dusty intersection along the back roads of Benton County, against Franklin High School of Portland. If Bellfountain should win, just one game separated it from the first chance in the tournament's history for a B League team—the state's classification for its smallest high schools—to win the overall state championship.

To advance this far in the tournament was a history-making achievement in itself for the small community of Bellfountain. With just 27 students, it was one of the smallest high schools in the state, yet it had already won the Benton County championship, the four-county District 16 tournament, and the Oregon State B League title before advancing to the semi-finals, where it would compete with two teams from Oregon's A League, the state's classification for its largest high schools. Yet in spite of the team's "Giant Killer" accomplishments so far, the odds facing Bellfountain as it prepared to battle these huge schools seemed insurmountable.

From its enrollment of 27 students, Bellfountain fielded a team of just eight boys, making it the smallest team in the tournament in numbers as well as in stature. Essentially, the team relied on its five starters; lose one of those starters to fouls, injury, or illness, and in most cases the game was lost. In contrast, the opponent they faced in this game, Franklin High School, could boast of not only a student population of more than 2,100 students—almost 80 times that of Bellfountain—but also a team of greater size and depth.

As a result, Bellfountain was the dark horse, the long shot, the underdog, and spectators had admired the team throughout the tournament. "Bellfountain, known throughout the state as [the Giant Killers]," noted that year's Willamette University yearbook, "was the crowd's favorite team."

It was an admiration aroused, perhaps, from the fact that Bellfountain seemed to dream of doing the impossible, of accomplishing feats beyond its limits, and the team's miraculous victories against overwhelming odds seemed to inspire others with hopes for their own personal miracles. But no matter what the reason for their crowd appeal, these eight young men from the back roads of Benton County were proving to be an inspiration in a time when the country was locked in the throes of the Great Depression.

Harry Wallace

And so when Bill Lemmon, Bellfountain's coach, brought his small, inspirational team— nicknamed the "Bells" by area sportswriters— onto the crowded basketball court at Willamette University, newspaper reporters scrambled to get the best camera angle, flash bulbs on cameras popped, and the crowd stood and roared as the Bells hustled to their bench.

The captain of the team and one of its stars was 5-foot 10-inch Harrison ("Harry") Wallace, the team's field general. An excellent dribbler and ball handler as well as one of the best shots on the team, Wallace was the man who brought the ball down the court, set up the offense, and ran the plays. "Are you nervous about playing this game?" someone asked him. "A little anxious," Harry said, "but not nervous."

The team's other star was 6-foot center Richard Kessler. Strong and agile with long arms and big hands, the husky Kessler could out-run almost everybody else on the team and out-jump opponents who were inches taller than he was. In addition, he had uncanny timing while reaching for the center jump, which took place after each score.

Richard Kessler

Another speedster was 5-foot 6-inch forward Stanley Buckingham, the shortest starter on the squad. With his red hair flopping wildly, Stan could arc long shots over the outstretched arms of much taller defenders.

At the other forward position was Stan's best friend and the only junior on the squad, 5-foot 7-inch Clifford Larkin, a good outside shooter.

The fourth senior on the team was Stan's brother, 5-foot 9-inch Frank Buckingham. Frank, the other guard and a terrific defender, was improving with each game. Rounding out the eight-man team were sophomore substitutes Lynn Hinton, Norman Humphrey, and John Key.

After Bellfountain's entrance, Franklin coach Charles "Chappie" King brought his Quakers onto the court accompanied by modest applause.

Then the two teams—tiny Bellfountain and giant Franklin—took their positions in the center of the basketball court, and on that 19th day of March in 1937, the semi-final game of the Oregon State High School Basketball Tournament began.

The referee tossed the ball into the air, and a frantic scuffle followed. Kessler tipped the ball to a teammate, but Franklin soon gained control and Bob Oliver scored. At the center jump, Bellfountain again controlled the ball but was unable to score. After Franklin came down the court, Manley Miles dropped in a basket to make the score 4-0.

This was probably when Franklin's players began their taunting, a tactic that involved using belittling talk to distract opponents in a 1930s version of today's "trash talk." The name-calling had worked earlier against Eugene High School, the tournament favorite that Franklin had defeated to gain an unexpected berth in the semi-finals. (In contrast, the tournament program pointed out that "The [Bellfountain] team plays exceptionally clean basketball.")

Stanley Buckingham

But when Franklin's players called Harry Wallace an obscene name, the ever-calm Wallace responded by dropping in one of his long bombs. Then after Kessler once again controlled the center jump, Stan Buckingham dribbled in for the basket. The first quarter ended with the score 4-4. While the Franklin players knew they were in the game of their lives, Bellfountain probably felt this was a game they could win.

Slowly the two teams settled down. But in the second quarter when Franklin's Oliver put the Quakers ahead 9-6 by rebounding and scoring on a missed free throw by teammate Robert Towne, it was Franklin's last basket for a long time. Bellfountain began dominating the backboards, stealing passes, controlling the center jump, playing flawless defense, and sprinting up and down the court while passing the ball so effectively that it rarely touched the floor.

After Kessler pumped in two shots, the Bells took a 16-9 halftime lead and were never challenged again. Franklin scored only two baskets in the second half, and to the approval of the throng of roaring fans, the game ended in a 39-13 Bellfountain victory that put the Giant Killers one win away from an unprecedented championship.

But before that chapter of the story unfolds, it's necessary to learn how a basketball team from such a small school could reach this pinnacle of success, to know who was responsible for instilling in these kids the seemingly impossible dream of winning a state championship as well as producing the confidence to achieve it. Some of the answers lie in the community of Bellfountain as well as with the people who made it their home.

Willamette University gym in Salem,
site of the state high school championship tournaments in the 1930s

The town of Bellfountain in the 1930s

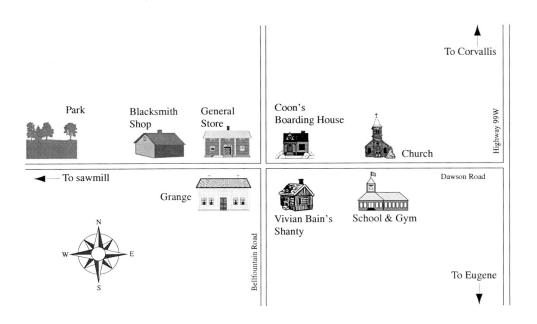

The Town of Bellfountain

S ome of the earliest recorded memories of Bellfountain stretch back to at least the 1880s and 1890s, a time when Ethel Mack attended school in the small Benton County town and later taught at small rural schools in the same area. "In those days," she said, "when there were no telephones, radios, televisions, no automobiles, and the roads were bad in winter, people in rural areas were more isolated than they are today."

It was, she said, a time of "close association between teacher and pupil— the walks through the woods in spring time, picking wild flowers or wild strawberries, and all the many joys of childhood in the country. The rural school child of the 1890s had something, infinitely precious, indefinable, something I wouldn't exchange for many more tangible advantages."

With the exception of a few phones, radios, and cars, Bellfountain in the 1930s was much like Ethel Mack's description of the rural 1890s—a small village clustered around two dusty bisecting roads, its people earning their living from logging and farming and millwork. On the northwest corner of that intersection stood Likens and Key General Merchandise Store, which included a Standard Oil gas pump on the front porch. Near the store was a blacksmith's shop, and across the street and west of the corner stood the Grange Hall.

Mrs. Coon's boarding house (left) and Bellfountain church

Nearby was the Bellfountain church, which had been a mainstay in the area since the 1800s, and which still had an age-old, spire-topped steeple. Just west of the church and on the same side of the street was Mr. and Mrs. Coon's boarding house, a two-story structure with four bedrooms upstairs and the "bathrooms" outside.

Across the street from the boarding house was the shanty of John Vivian Bain, the caretaker and school custodian. And up the hill and east of his home stood the heart of the town—its school and gymnasium.

Built about 1908, the school housed twelve grades in five classrooms, two of which were used for the high school. Its gymnasium, located next door, was built in about 1913 when Bellfountain's families decided that their children needed some athletic endeavor other than football and baseball, which required more students than were enrolled in the school.

Basketball soon became *the* game in town, and in the gym's early years the court was illuminated for night games with the headlights of Model T's that were pulled into open doors at the end of the building. By the 1930s, however, a gasoline generator supplied the lights, two potbelly stoves furnished the heat, and a small building standing 60 or 70 feet away provided wood-heated showers.

Perhaps it was because of Bellfountain's seclusion or its lack of modern conveniences that special bonds of affection developed between teachers, parents, and students. Throw into this mix a teacher and coach of exceptional ability, and great things can happen. That's what occurred in Bellfountain when into this pristine country setting came Kenneth Litchfield, a man filled with the zeal of youth, an attitude that anything was possible, and the commitment and ability to inspire and lead.

Bellfountain school and gymnasium

According to local historian Marlene McDonald, in the early years of Bellfountain School, some students who were not content with studying took up the art of shooting spit wads. Their accuracy was uncanny. Some were able to dot the periods at the ends of sentences on the blackboard. In addition, on Halloween some students would sneak up to the school's belfry and remove the bell's clapper as a prank.

Ken and Frances Litchfield and their car Bennie

The Arrival of Coach Litchfield

In September of 1929, driving his Franklin automobile (named "Bennie") with the rumble seat pulled wide open and dust swirling behind, Kenneth Litchfield turned west off the main road that connected Eugene with Corvallis and drove the three miles to the little community of Bellfountain. As he entered the town, he passed the school and gym on his left, the church on his right, then pulled into a parking area in front of the two-story Coon's boarding house, which was often used by new teachers. After being shown to his upstairs bedroom, Litchfield returned to his car and unloaded his belongings, including a .22 rifle.

One morning before the opening of school, the 23-year-old Litchfield grabbed his .22 and plodded down the stairs and out onto the front porch of the boarding house. Aiming his rifle at the bell atop the school house, he shot a couple of rounds, making the school bell ping with the zinging bullets. The Litchfield era of teaching and coaching had begun at Bellfountain School.

Born in Yaquina City and raised in Portland where he attended Washington High School, Litchfield went on to achieve a distinguished career at Willamette University in Salem. He played on the varsity basketball team for three years, became captain of the tennis team, participated in track, served as student body president, and eventually earned degrees in law and political science. Obviously, Litchfield was a young man overflowing with ambition. He was also a leader, an organizer, a man blessed with a strong intellect and compassion as well as high values and principles.

Ken Litchfield

Yet when he graduated from Willamette in 1929 with the idea of becoming a practicing lawyer, the Great Depression made opportunities scarce. So when he learned that Bellfountain needed a principal, teacher, and coach—a position that might be paid in money, scrip, or commodities—Litchfield applied for the job. For the next seven years he would pour his unbounded enthusiasm and energy into the community.

The Young Giant Killers

Soon after his arrival, Litchfield walked into the Bellfountain gym and found a group of fourth- and fifth-graders playing basketball. He undoubtedly noted their lack of structure and fundamentals necessary to play the game. After winning the team's respect, even affection, he began the long, slow process of organizing them. This was the beginning of the "Giant Killers" basketball team. These future Giant Killers all lived within several miles of the school, and all of them used the gym as their hangout.

Richard Kessler lived in one of the unpainted houses in the center of town. His father worked as a tree trimmer in a large prune orchard.

Harry Wallace, the eldest of five children, lived at the Westmiller Sawmill about four miles west of the school. His father worked at the mill as a pond monkey who was in charge of getting the logs into the mill.

Alvah Hinton's father was a bookkeeper at the sawmill.

Cliff Larkin lived on a 160-acre farm about a mile from school, where his parents grew grain, wheat, and hay as well as raised pigs, milk cows, and horses.

Frank and Stan Buckingham's parents were long-time area farmers. The boys spent their hours doing chores, walking or running to school, playing basketball, and studying.

Possessing a great understanding of the game and its subtleties, Litchfield knew how to organize young players as a team as well as how to get the best performance from each individual. He noticed Harry Wallace's leadership capabilities and placed him at one guard position, a controlling spot for the team. The other guard was Alvah Hinton, Wallace's close buddy.

Frank Buckingham

At the center position Litchfield placed the husky Richard Kessler, and at the two forward positions he put redheaded Stan Buckingham and Cliff Larkin, who were best friends. The few remaining players became substitutes, including Frank Buckingham, the best of the lot and Stan's brother.

The Litchfields as newlyweds, 1930

During this time, one significant event occurred in Litchfield's life as well as in the community when his fiancé, Frances McGilvra, filled with the same kind of enthusiasm and energy as Ken, arrived in Bellfountain in 1930 after graduating that spring as a biology major from Willamette University. Soon after her arrival and her marriage to Ken, the two became not only Bellfountain's high school faculty and coaching staff, but also community leaders who would serve as major influences on the young Giant Killers.

Over the next few years, Litchfield instilled the fundamentals of the game into his young team. He taught the boys how to pass, pivot, shoot the two-handed set shot (the "long bomb" shot later replaced

The Bellfountain gym,
where Ken Litchfield taught his young team the fundamentals of the game

by the one-handed push shot and the jump shot), and the underhand free throw (shot with both hands holding the sides of the ball, which was lowered between the knees and then arced upwards toward the hoop).

One of the most important lessons Litchfield taught his team was not to foul opposing players. The logic behind it was clear: On a small team, every player was so important that losing just one starter to foul trouble likely meant losing the game. (In those days, a player who received four fouls was out of the game.) Like Litchfield's other lessons, this one took hold with the young team and helped set the players on a course for success.

Liked and respected by the parents and children of the community, Litchfield molded, shaped, and nurtured his team, and his involvement and influence stretched far beyond the basketball court. He inspired hope and a competitive attitude in the age of the Great Depression, becoming a friend and even a father figure to some in the community. He ate meals in his players' homes, and families celebrated with him when his wife Frances gave birth to their daughter Carol.

Then in 1933 Litchfield had the opportunity to see how his training was developing when the basketball coach at Philomath, a much larger neighboring community to the north, asked Litchfield if he could muster a team from Bellfountain to play Philomath's junior varsity. Litchfield said all he had was a group of eighth graders, but he would be willing to let them play. The overconfident Philomath coach accepted, evidently thinking it wouldn't be much of a match.

To everyone's amazement, including Bellfountain's, Litchfield's eighth graders won the game 40-10. Looking back at this game years later, Harry Wallace thought it might have been one of the sparks that helped the team believe they could beat larger schools, even on the other team's home court.

Ken Litchfield and his young Bellfountain team

24

A Different Game

In the 1930s Litchfield's teams played a style of basketball different from today's game. The primary difference was the center jump rule, the means of putting the ball back into play after each score: After either team made a basket, both teams returned to the center of the court, where the referee tossed the ball into the air, and each team's center tried to out-jump the other in an attempt to tip the ball to his teammates, who stood outside a six-foot circle that surrounded the two centers. (The same practice today is limited mostly to the beginning of the game and the second half.)

"It was the only part of basketball where actual bodily contact was countenanced by the rules," said one sports writer of the time. "For that reason alone it was colorful, spectacular, and spectator-appealing."

In spite of its appeal, most of the nation's coaches favored doing away with the center jump rule because it gave the advantage to larger schools with taller players while seriously handicapping smaller schools with shorter athletes. In fact, J. Craig Ruby of Illinois and George F. Veenker of Michigan, two famous coaches of the day, calculated that the team that controlled the center jump had an advantage of six to ten points in any game.

Consequently, elaborate offenses and defenses were designed around this center jump method of play, and the game's tempo as well as its scores were drastically slowed down. It was common for high school games to end up with scores in the 30s, 20s, and even lower.

In fact, numerous rules, types of shots, and playing styles of the day worked against the small schools simply because they usually lacked coaches who could teach the latest techniques. Coach Litchfield, however, was an exception. He not only knew about advancements in the game because he had used them while playing at Willamette University, but also possessed the ability to teach these skills to the young Giant Killers.

Another marked difference in the 1930s occurred when the Oregon High School Athletic Association divided the state's high schools into two leagues, A and B. All high schools with enrollments of 150 students or less were in the B League, while those with higher enrollments were classed in the A League. The A League consisted of 67 schools while the B League was made up of 194 schools.

Bellfountain belonged to the Benton County Conference—along with Alsea, Philomath, Lobster, and Monroe—that was in District 16, the Willamette Division, which consisted of four counties and 42 small high schools. Beginning with the 1934-35 season when they were sophomores, the Giant Killers would dominate their B League conference for the next three seasons.

The 1934-35 Season

With the instructional guidance and inspiration of Coach Litchfield and the leadership of young Harry Wallace, the mostly-sophomore Bellfountain team formed itself into a cohesive unit during the 1934-35 season and won the conference championship by beating Monroe, Alsea, Philomath and Lobster.

As the Benton County B League representative to the District 16 Playoffs held in Albany, Bellfountain played its way through teams from Linn, Lane, and Lincoln counties to earn a berth in the B League semi-final game against Oakridge, which defeated Bellfountain by a score of 26-12.

One reason for Bellfountain's loss was Oakridge's outstanding 6-foot 4-inch Laddie Gale, who later played for the University of Oregon's "Tall Firs," a team that won the NCAA basketball championship. The young Bells learned a few tricks from one of the best players in the state, made a comeback in the consolation game by beating Toledo, and settled for a third place finish in their first test at tournament play.

The 1934-35 Bellfountain team and its trophy for third place at the District 16 Tournament.

Top row (from left to right): Frank Buckingham, Dewey Cole,
Elmer Likens, Alvah Hinton, Ken Litchfield

Bottom row: Harry Wallace, Sherman Key, Verlin Post,
Richard Kessler, Howard Elston, Stanley Buckingham

The 1935-36 Season

T he conference is the same as it was last year," the Philomath newspaper reported in November of 1935, "with Monroe, Alsea, Bellfountain, Lobster, and Philomath." The article went on to report that Alsea and Monroe had new coaches and that it would be difficult to figure out who would win the conference. It failed to mention, however, that Bellfountain had finished third in the previous season's District Tournament and that its entire team was returning.

Before conference play began, Bellfountain was scheduled to play a series of pre-season games. In the first of these, Bellfountain defeated the Corvallis Shoemakers, a team sponsored by a shoe business, by a score of 44-19. In its next game against Harrisburg, which had a student enrollment of more than 100, Coach Litchfield probably wondered what in the world he had unearthed, for his Bellfountain team won 64-7. When Harrisburg asked for a rematch, Bellfountain drubbed them again, this time 54-18.

The next three pre-season games, however, matched Bellfountain against much larger schools, starting with the Willamette University freshman team in Salem and following with Corvallis High School (more than 500 students) and University High School in Eugene (more than 200 students). These three games looked like a road to disaster. Consequently, the Bells' 27-24 win over Willamette's freshmen was an upset, though their next opponent, the Corvallis High School Spartans, promised to be an even tougher team.

With 6-foot 4-inch Stu Warren playing center for Corvallis, the home team Spartans seemed to have the six- to ten-point advantage so often claimed by the taller team. But as the game unfolded, the Bells employed a fast-breaking offense and a hard-to-penetrate zone defense.

Clifford Larkin

The team's passing was so good, Cliff Larkin said later, that sometimes when the Bells came down the court on offense, the team didn't have to dribble. "We would pass the ball so efficiently," he said, "that it would never touch the floor." As a result, after Corvallis led briefly in the first quarter, Bellfountain led at halftime 15-8.

In the second half, the Bells' superb ball handling continued, enabling Bellfountain to hold a 23-12 lead when the third quarter ended. Then the Spartans made a surge, closing the gap to four points with five minutes left to play, and Coach Litchfield called a time out. He wanted his team to stall for the last five minutes. (In the 1930s, stalling was an acceptable strategy that permitted a team of good ball handlers to maintain a lead after getting a few points ahead.) When play resumed, Corvallis was almost unable to get its hands on the ball. Harry Wallace scored the only basket in the last five minutes, putting the Bells ahead for good at 25-19, and keeping intact the team's undefeated record in their tough pre-season schedule. Nevertheless, they next faced University High School in Eugene, another A League team.

Playing on the home court of University High, Bellfountain scored the first 14 points of the contest and led at the half 16-6. "Wallace Leads Bellfountain Quintet to 35-24 Win Over University High," announced a late-December headline in the Eugene *Register Guard.*

Less than two weeks later, a second game was played between the two teams, this time in the Bellfountain gym, and the Bells beat them 44-14. The University High School annual for 1936 conveniently left out these scores with Bellfountain, which ended its pre-season with a record of 7-0.

Riding this wave of victories, the Bells entered their conference schedule in January, and their winning ways continued. They began by defeating Alsea 47-20, and the next week traveled the 30 graveled miles into the heart of the Coast Range to play Lobster, a school even smaller than Bellfountain.

The Lobster gym was a big wooden structure with a low ceiling. A classroom was at one end while a stage with four rows of bleachers was at the other. A generator provided electricity for the lights, heat came from a large wood stove, and the gym's walls served as the out-of-bounds. The Lobster fans, rooting from the stage's bleachers, were mostly from one family named Hendrix. In fact, of the team's five players—the high school had an enrollment of only eight or nine students—four were brothers or cousins of the Hendrix clan, including 6-foot 2-inch Lloyd Hendrix and his 6-foot, 220-pound cousin Fred.

The Hendrixes, it seemed, had figured out how to guard Richard Kessler, the Bells' star center. Even though Kessler could be rough under the backboards, the larger Hendrixes, especially big Fred, dominated the area under the basket, making it tough for Bellfountain to get through. In addition, Harry Wallace discovered it was tough arcing the ball over the large Hendrix boys in a gym with a low ceiling. But even though Lobster held Kessler to just five points in that game, the Bells won decisively, 31-8. With its unbeaten record intact, Bellfountain next faced Philomath.

"The Philomath squad is going into the conflict with a spirit and a determination that will make Bellfountain work if they want to win the game," Philomath's *Benton County Review* reported, "[and] a lot of people… think that Philomath has a good chance to take the game." But Bellfountain led at the half 19-2 and won the game 39-11. Next up was Monroe, a high school of almost 100 students located 10 miles northeast of Bellfountain.

Monroe gave the Bells a scare, taking the lead early, falling behind only 16-9 at the half, and pulling within one point several different times. Still, the close game ended 26-19 with the Bells on top.

The next week at the Bellfountain gym, the Bells faced a rematch with Lobster. The Hendrix clan played a good game, though again Bellfountain won, this time 34-20.

In the following weeks, Bellfountain defeated Falls City 23-18, Philomath 28-12, and Monroe 42-28. Standing out during this streak, which left the team with a 15-0 record, was the sharp shooting of Harry Wallace, Richard Kessler, and Stan Buckingham.

Another significant factor in the team's success, however, took place off the court, and that was Bellfountain's strong community support for its basketball players. Many in the community attended all the away games, and those who couldn't travel still gathered around their radios to hear the outcome. As a result, the special bonds of affection between coach, school, and community continued to grow.

Meanwhile, up the road, Corvallis High School of the A League was playing its best basketball of the season. In spite of their earlier loss to Bellfountain, the Spartans were undefeated in league play, and now these league-leading teams, two of the best high school teams in the state, clashed again in February at the Bellfountain gym.

It must have seemed strange for the big Corvallis team and its supporters to travel south 30 miles from a college town and business center to

Bellfountain, where they found a general store with a gas pump on its front porch and the high school with its small gym and outdoor showers. When the Corvallis contingent pulled into Bellfountain's dirt parking lot, the gym's two wood stoves were fired up and radiating heat. The gasoline generator was putt-putting away, keeping the lights burning. The spectators were crowded into the tiny gym, leaving barely enough room to stand. Then Coach Litchfield brought in his undefeated Bells, and "Mush" Torsen his league-leading Spartans.

The teams took their positions at mid-court. Richard Kessler and Stewart Warren faced off in the center jump circle, with Warren's four-inch height advantage making the difference. The game soon turned into a defensive struggle with close shots difficult to come by. So Bellfountain tried long shots and only rarely passed the ball to Kessler inside. The Spartans, meanwhile, had their own problems. Because of the Bells' tight defense, Corvallis missed several set-up shots and committed several turnovers. At the end of the first half, the score was deadlocked 9-9.

In the second half, the Bells continued to emphasize a tight defense and long shooting. The player that turned things around for the Spartans was Elmo Crockett, who scored most of his eight points in the second half, leading Corvallis to a 22-16 victory and handing the Bells their first defeat of the season.

Even though Bellfountain hoped to rebound from this defeat, Harry Wallace fell ill and missed the next week's game against Falls City. His absence was a serious handicap, and Bellfountain lost its second game in a row, this time 25-11.

When Wallace returned in time for the Benton County B League Tournament, however, Bellfountain clinched the county title by easily defeating Lobster 50-23. The team then set its sights on the district tournament held in Corvallis, where the victor of the four-county, eight -team clash would advance to the state tournament at Willamette University in Salem.

In the first games of the 1936 district tournament, which was held in mid-March, spectators paid the cost of admission (15 cents for students, 25 cents for everyone else), filed in to the Corvallis gym, and watched Bellfountain down Pleasant Hill 25-17 in the first round, then Newport 37-21 in the second to advance to the championship game against Thurston High School of Springfield. Even though the title game was close, Bellfountain led throughout to take a 19-13 victory and earn its first trip to the state championship.

Bellfountain's 1935-36 basketball team
Top row (from left): Ken Litchfield, Stanley Buckingham, Harry Wallace, Frank Buckingham, Richard Kessler, Clifford Larkin
Bottom row: Arden Stahl, Dewey Cole, Lyle King, Elmer Likens, John Key
Missing: starting guard Alvah Hinton

The 1936 State Tournament

T he program for the Seventeenth Annual State High School Basketball Tournament predicted some possible tournament winners: Salem, the host team; Astoria, the defending champion; Franklin or Benson of Portland; Tillamook or Corvallis. But not a word was written about the possibility of Bellfountain or any of the other three B League district champions winning the A tournament; after all, no B League team had ever done it before.

Because of its tough schedule and the fact that it had lost only twice, Bellfountain was the favorite in its first game against Umapine, a contest played in front of a record crowd of more than 3,600 spectators. With Richard Kessler and Harry Wallace combining to score 16 points in the first half and 28 in the game, and with the entire team demonstrating why *The Oregon Statesman* called the Bells a club of "smooth ball handlers," Bellfountain defeated Umapine 35-15.

In the following game against Myrtle Creek for the B League championship, the Bells went out front early and stayed there, winning the title by a score of 31-22. "Ken Litchfield's hustling band of ball tossers," was how the *Salem Capital Journal* described the team.

Perhaps even more important than the team's ball handling, however, was the fact that they committed not a single personal foul during the entire game, a situation that gave them a decided scoring advantage at the free throw line. And once Bellfountain clinched the state B League basketball championship, it proceeded into the semi-finals of the A League tournament against its old nemesis, Corvallis, which so far in the tournament had beaten last year's champion and proven itself almost unstoppable. Nevertheless, for a B League team to make it into the A League semi-finals was a milestone in state basketball history, and the Bells quickly became crowd favorites.

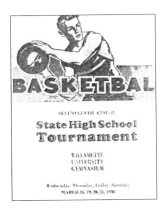

Willamette University gymnasium,
as it appeared at the time of the 1936 state tournament

"Bellfountain's fighting spirit," said *The Oregon Statesman*, "was the admiration of every tournament fan." Of course, the Bellfountain community, both at the tournament and back home, was foremost in that admiration, especially when the Bells once again faced off against the Spartans.

Because Spartan center Stewart Warren towered four inches over the 6-foot Kessler, Corvallis coach "Mush" Torsen must have realized that Warren would be the key to his team's success. He also knew that Corvallis had to strike fast and sure because Bellfountain would respond quickly.

The starting five of Bellfountain and Corvallis gathered in the center of the court for the center jump. Stu Warren easily took control, tipping the ball to a teammate. It was the beginning of Warren's domination of the center jump during the entire first quarter, and Corvallis jumped out to a 10 point lead. Under the leadership of Harry Wallace, however, Bellfountain responded to the challenge, and from the second quarter to the end of the game the Bells matched the Spartans point for point. But they couldn't make up for Corvallis's early lead, and the game ended with a 34-25 Corvallis win.

With their quest for the A League championship over, Bellfountain set about winning the third place trophy in the consolation game against McLoughlin High School. In this final game of the season, the Bells romped. Wallace scored 11 points; Kessler dropped in eight but suffered from foul trouble and had to leave the game in the third quarter. His replacement was the seldom seen substitute Elmer Likens, who in spite of his inexperience still contributed six points of his own. Bellfountain took the game 29-17 and placed third in the tournament, while Corvallis went on to pound Franklin 34-20 in the championship finals.

Elmer Likens

The Bells came away with most of the "booty," reported *The Oregon Statesman.* "Bellfountain got the handsome bronze B trophy, the gilt third place [A League] trophy and to the boy who generated his team through four days of championship play, Harrison Wallace, went the sportsmanship trophy." In addition, the All-State B League team included Bellfountain's Stan Buckingham, Richard Kessler, and Harry Wallace.

Alvah Hinton

After the team arrived home, it joined other successful teams from the area in attending awards banquets held in their honor in both Corvallis and Bellfountain. These were evenings of eating, music, and praise for the teams' achievements. During both banquets, perhaps only a few people noticed that some of the Bells had their eyes covetously fixed on the first place trophy that Corvallis High School had won at the state tournament—because with only guard Alvah Hinton graduating in the spring, four starters would return for the 1937 season.

A Change of Coaches

The small community of Bellfountain returned to normal after the fantastic success of its basketball team. Farmers awaited their harvests, loggers continued cutting trees with spring boards and two-man felling saws, and mills buzzed with the labor of turning timber into lumber. Mrs. Coon tended to her boarders; the Bellfountain general store noticed an increase in business; the pastor of the community church prepared his sermons with a new optimism; John Vivian Bain, school custodian, worked at keeping the school clean and in working order; and the children returned to classes and their studies. Yet things were also changing in the small town.

Ken & Frances Litchfield

One change that would have a big impact on the small community was that even as Ken and Frances Litchfield tended their daughter Carol—Frances had resigned from her teaching position at the end of the 1932-33 school year to become a full time mother—they also struggled with the loss of a a child to an institution, for Frances had recently given birth to a son with Down's Syndrome. Once the Litchfields decided to send their son, Donald Kenneth Litchfield, to Fairview institution in Salem, they grappled with the consequences of their decision. (This situation, which occurred before the end of basketball season, undoubtedly affected the team as well as its coach.)

Another change emerged when the school at Shedd, Oregon, offered Litchfield the position of school superintendent, a job that paid more at a school with twice the enrollment of Bellfountain. And so in the summer of 1936, with the Litchfields heartbroken from the loss of their new-born son, Ken accepted the new job and moved with Frances and Carol to Shedd.

Left without a teacher and coach, the community of Bellfountain went searching for a replacement. At Willamette University they found 24-year-old Burton C. "Bill" Lemmon, who had graduated that spring and who was eager to take over where Litchfield had left off.

A former All-State basketball player on a state championship team in Tacoma, Washington, and a three-year player for Willamette's varsity, the newly-married Lemmon began his job in September as the principal of both the elementary and high schools; as a teacher of mathematics, history, typing,

mechanical drawing, and physical geography; and, of course, as the coach of the third best basketball team in the state the previous year. As it turned out, the hiring of Lemmon fulfilled his dream of becoming a coach while providing Bellfountain with an extraordinary man to lead a promising team.

Because he recognized the superb potential of the Bellfountain team and understood the players still loved their former coach, Lemmon didn't tamper with the well-functioning unit. In

Bill Lemmon

essence, he took over a team that possessed the attitude and skills of winners, and he simply added to what the players already knew. Even though this was certain to be a time of transition, it was fortunate for Bellfountain that one exceptional coach followed another in this remote part of Oregon.

The team Bill Lemmon inherited from Ken Litchfield (shown here with his 1935-36 team) included four of the five starters that placed third at state in 1936: Richard Kessler (far left), Clifford Larkin (second from left), Harry Wallace (second from right), and Stanley Buckingham (far right). Frank Buckingham (fourth from right) would complete Lemmon's starting lineup.

The 27 students and two teachers of Bellfountain High School, 1936-37

The 1936-37 Season

In November of 1936 when Coach Lemmon announced the beginning of basketball practice, practically the entire team from the historic 1936 tournament showed up, and Lemmon soon had his eight-man roster for the season: Richard Kessler at center, Stanley Buckingham and Clifford Larkin at forwards; Harrison Wallace and Frank Buckingham at guards. The substitutes, who wouldn't see much playing time but who were still vital parts of the team, were John Key, Lynn Hinton, and Norman Humphrey. Once the games began, the Bells picked up right where they'd left off at last spring's state tournament—by winning.

First they crunched the Salem Crunchers, a business-sponsored team, 45-19. Then they hammered Harrisburg 72-15 before taking on St. Mary's of Eugene with its 6-foot 6-inch center Archie Marshik, a team they man-handled 37-17. The following game, however, was against traditional foe Corvallis in the only meeting of the season between the two Benton County rivals.

Corvallis was not the same team it had been a year earlier. They had neither their tall center Stuart Warren nor their All-State player Merle Kruger, who had been voted the state tournament's outstanding player the previous spring. But they still had a great coach in "Mush" Torsen as well as starters

Elmo Crockett and big Bill Blackledge, who had been moved to center because of his height. In other words, Corvallis was not a team to be taken for granted.

The inter-county contest was exciting from the first center jump, and Kessler and Wallace led the Bells to an 11-2 first quarter advantage. In the second quarter, the Spartans fought back and at halftime trailed by only five points. By the end of the third period, spectators knew they were watching a rivalry at its best, with the Bells staying ahead of the Spartans 18-17.

In the fourth quarter, Bellfountain scored on a basket and a free throw to increase their lead to 21-17. The real excitement began with four minutes left in the game when Elmo Crockett, who had been held scoreless up to this point, was finally able to score, bringing the Spartans to within two points of the Bells, 21-19.

Then Bellfountain began a stall. Torsen sent in Avery, who immediately fouled Frank Buckingham. With two minutes remaining, Frank missed his free throw, and as Reish grabbed the rebound for the Spartans, Arden Hearing "snuck" back to the Spartan basket. Reish immediately threw a long pass to Hearing who tossed in the "cripple," an uncontested basket. With the game tied at 21 and less then a minute to play, Elmo Crockett tossed in the winning basket, giving Corvallis a 23-21 win.

Bellfountain may have lost the game but not its spirit. Except for the next game against the Willamette University Frosh team, when Kessler tossed in the last basket for a 21-20 victory, the games played over the following weeks were easy victories for the talented Bellfountain five as they downed in succession Shedd (Ken Litchfield's new school), the Salem Ramblers (a business-sponsored team), Monroe (a conference game), Shedd (again), and Alsea (another conference game, which Bellfountain won 48-4). These victories drew the attention of *The Oregon Statesman* sports writer Paul Hauser, who called Richard Kessler, then averaging almost 15 points per game and shooting with almost 60 percent accuracy from the field, a real basketball treasure.

In the Bells' next non-conference match-up at the gym of an improved St. Mary's team, the game went much as predicted, with the Bells leading 16-8 at the half. But then early in the third period, Richard Kessler fouled out, and 6-foot 6-inch Archie Marshik began dominating both the center jump and the backboards for St. Mary's.

By the end of the third period, the score was tied at 22. In the fourth quarter, first one team and then the other took the lead. Despite St. Mary's height advantage, the Bells kept the game close, but with just three minutes left Schimel of St. Mary's sank a long basket to tie the score at 29. A minute later Marshik, who totaled 10 points for the game, tipped in a teammate's missed shot for the winning score.

With their second loss of the season hanging over their heads, the Bells next faced Salem High School, perhaps the largest in the state with more than 2,300 students.

Driving their Franklins, Olds, and Model T Fords, the Bellfountain five and their supporters took to the graveled roads and drove out to the main highway, heading north towards Salem, Oregon's capital city. After they arrived at Salem's two-story high school, a building so big that the gymnasium was upstairs, the Bellfountain contingent tromped upstairs and emerged in a huge gym with rows and rows of screaming students and spectators waiting for them and cheering on their Salem Vikings. It was, *The Oregon Statesman* reported later, the "largest crowd to watch a Salem High basketball game this season." Bill Lemmon, however, reminded his team that "it was just another game," and the well-coached Bells got off to a quick start.

Harry Wallace, not intimidated at all by the large, unfriendly crowd, was in his element in the first period. With Kessler controlling the center jump, the ball usually ended up in Wallace's hands. Then, with the precision of a Swiss watch maker, Wallace's set shots found their mark. Yet Salem still managed to keep up with Wallace's exacting pace.

Tom Medley, the Vikings' top scorer, had a tough time breaking through the Bells' tight zone defense, but his teammate Sumner Gallaher took up the slack, scoring nine points on four field goals and a free throw. At halftime Bellfountain led 12-10.

In the third quarter of this fierce battle, both teams turned in a thrilling performance, with the lead changing hands six times. For every point Salem scored, Bellfountain responded with one of its own. Stan Buckingham made a shot from the side to put the Bells in the lead 17-16, only to lose it again on Salem's next offensive drive. Then the steady, reliable Kessler shot one in from the foul line that gave the Bells a 19-18 lead at the end of the third period.

The fourth period was a stalemate with neither team scoring until Larkin missed a shot, and Kessler scored on the rebound to make the score 21-18. Then, with 30 seconds left on the clock, Gallaher scored a basket for the Vikings, but the Bells hung on for a 21-20 win.

The following week, the Salem Vikings and their crowd of supporters crowded into the Bellfountain gym in a rematch. With spectators packed tight in the stands, the doors at both ends of the gym were left wide open so the overflow crowd could watch. It was a spirited contest that saw Salem challenge the Bells often, but Bellfountain won the game 29-23.

"Of all the high schools Salem has played," Paul Hauser wrote later in *The Oregon Statesman*, "[Bellfountain] is the only one which has beaten Salem twice. Corvallis, Astoria, Eugene, Medford, McMinnville, Tillamook, and the Willamette Frosh couldn't do it."

Bellfountain seemed to have built up a head of steam—especially Kessler and Wallace—and no one seemed able to stop them, though it was difficult to say who was emerging as the team's brightest star. "It's pretty hard to choose between Dick and Harry," Lemmon said. "Dick is high scorer but Wallace runs the team."

In the final two games of the regular season, the Bells defeated Philomath 36-12 and the Willamette University Frosh 29-23. Then it was on to the conference tournament, where they beat Alsea 49-23 and Monroe 42-22. Finally, in the district tournament, they put away Shedd 49-15 and Thurston 34-23. With conference and district titles to its credit, Bellfountain once again headed for the State Basketball Tournament in Salem.

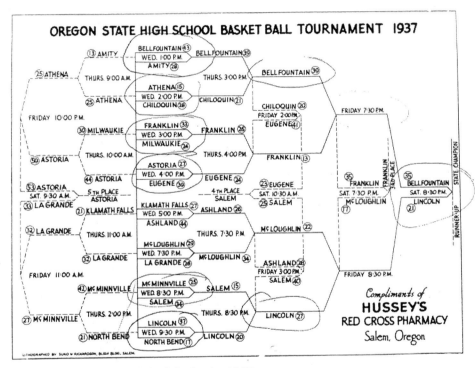

Schedule for the 1937 state tournament

The 1937 State Tournament

The championship teams from the state's 16 districts, along with their families and supporters, crowded into Salem. They filled the streets with their cars and the hotels with themselves. The majority of sports writers agreed that the A teams to be reckoned with were Eugene, Astoria, Franklin, and Lincoln, with Salem given an outside chance.

Most also predicted that Bellfountain—described in the tournament's program as a "little town...located somewhere in the hills of Benton County"—would win the state B trophy. When the tournament began, more than 2,000 fans were there to see Bellfountain play Amity in the first game.

At one o'clock sharp, the basketball was tossed into the air, and Richard Kessler and Amity's 6-foot 2-inch Bill Moddemeyer leaped in the center jump. Even though Amity had the height advantage, Kessler and teammates poured in 11 unanswered points. (This would be the last season for the center jump rule; on this same day, the National Rules Committee would approve the recommendation of the National Collegiate Basketball Coaches Association, which had voted 60-9 to eliminate the rule beginning with the following season.)

Amity shifted from a man-to-man to a zone defense but were still unable to contain the Bellfountain ball handlers. With his quickness, Kessler was often able to control the ball and make uncontested shots, and Bellfountain led 15-3 at the end of the first quarter and 20-11 at the half.

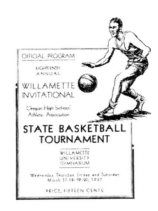

In the second half when Lemmon pulled Kessler and Stan Buckingham from the lineup for a rest on the bench, the one-handed shooting style of Amity's Wayne Giesy—the one-handed push shot was a novelty in the 1930s, though Giesy scored 13 points in this game—pulled Amity to within six points. Kessler and Buckingham went back into the game, and once again the Bells began to dominate.

Scoring from close range and breaking up the Amity offense were Kessler's specialties, and the Bells quickly scored nine more points while shutting out Amity. Wallace scored 10 points while Kessler's 20 made him the tournament's leading scorer for the day.

The rest of the games that day went according to prediction, especially for A League teams: Franklin beat Milwaukie 33-24, Salem toppled McMinnville, Lincoln thrashed North Bend, and Eugene dominated Astoria 39-27, leading many to believe that Eugene would win the championship. The winners of these games, as well as B League winners Bellfountain and Chiloquin, advanced to the next day's second round.

The first game of the next round, between the scrappy Chiloquin five from the Klamath Reservation and the expert ball handlers of Bellfountain, would determine the state B championship, and the winner would advance to the tournament's semi-finals to play for the A trophy.

Richard Kessler and teammates methodically and patiently outplayed and outscored the team from the reservation, leading at the half 24-9 and winning the game 39-21. Because of Wallace's accurate passing, Kessler scored 16 points under and around the basket, becoming the tournament's top scorer for the second day. Wallace, using his set shots, was also hot, dropping in 11 points.

With the state's B League championship settled, the A League teams resumed their quest for the trophy. And when Franklin defeated tourney favorite Eugene 26-24 and Lincoln beat Salem 20-15, it not only set up the semi-final match between Franklin and Bellfountain, and but also started predictions of a Portland sweep of first and second places.

That, of course, was before Bellfountain beat Franklin 39-13 the next day to become the first B League team ever to enter the state A League finals. In the other semi-final game, the Lincoln Railsplitters defeated McLoughlin High 27 to 22 and were now slated to play Bellfountain for the state championship game on Saturday, March 20, 1937. It was to be a game that would go down in Oregon basketball history.

[To] BELLFOUNTAIN BASKETBALL TEAM

GO GET EM WE ARE FOR YOU
SIX HUNDRED STRONG

[From] ASSOCIATED STUDENTS
CORVALLIS HIGH SCHOOL

–Western Union Telegram received by the
Bellfountain basketball team on the eve of their state championship game

The Championship Game

Even though it had reached the A League championship finals, the odds against Bellfountain appeared overwhelming. After all, Lincoln's enrollment was 1,728 students to Bellfountain's 27, and the Railsplitters' players stood inches taller than Bellfountain's, with center Bill Neill looming four inches above Richard Kessler. In addition, "Wee Dave" Wright, Lincoln's coach, knew a thing or two about defense. All in all, the odds of the smallest school in the tournament winning the championship were slim indeed. Nevertheless, the Bellfountain players were ready for the team's last and most important contest of what had already been a miraculous season.

In addition, the team had the advantage of Ken Litchfield and Bill Lemmon sitting together on the Bells' bench. The situation apparently resulted in an argument during a game. When asked about it, however, the coaches explained the disagreement involved Lemmon trying to give Litchfield the credit for the team's success while Litchfield insisted on giving Lemmon the credit. Evidently, Lemmon's regard for Litchfield was already well-known. Bill Lemmon, the tournament program noted, "is extremely modest, giving all the credit for his fine team to last year's Bellfountain coach Ken Litchfield."

And so with the two coaches putting the argument aside, the Bells went to work. They began the game as they had so many times before, with Wallace setting up the offense, passing the ball around the court to his teammates, then firing a bullet in to Kessler, in to the heart of Lincoln's vaunted defense. When Kessler scored, the crowd stood and roared.

After winning the center jump, Lincoln found itself pressured everywhere by Bellfountain's defenders. The Railsplitters' shot missed and Bellfountain rebounded, their passes coming down the court so fast and sure that the Railsplitters' heads swiveled back and forth in trying to follow the ball as it flashed past them. Then Wallace once again found Kessler for the score. Sportswriters' cameras clicked and their flashbulbs popped as the gym erupted in cheering at Bellfountain's 4-0 lead.

Once again Bill Neill beat Kessler at the center jump, this time tipping the ball to teammate Lee Sitton, one of the best guards in the state. Sitton dribbled into Lincoln's offensive zone, but Bellfountain seemed to be everywhere—arms outstretched, feet moving, keeping pace with Lincoln's plays and applying relentless pressure. Sitton shot and missed, then Neill and Hansen missed shots on successive rebounds. Finally, Bellfountain rebounded, and Wallace passed to Stan Buckingham, who was fouled and made the free throw for a 5-0 lead.

Lincoln won the center jump, and Lee Sitton took the ball down court, but Bellfountain intercepted a pass and scored. Losing the ball at the center jump again, Bellfountain badgered the Railsplitters at every turn, and at the end of the first quarter held a 9-4 lead.

The second quarter was similar to the first with Lincoln controlling the tip and the backboards, but missing numerous shots. Meanwhile, Bellfountain, spurred on by the enthusiastic crowd, caused turnovers, passed with pinpoint accuracy, fouled rarely, and scored from the free throw line as well as from the field to take an 18-8 halftime lead.

Something coach Wright said at halftime sparked his team because Lincoln's performance improved in the third quarter. Midway through the period the Railsplitters made their move, scoring five unanswered points, reducing Bellfountain's lead to 22-15. Then to start the fourth quarter, Lincoln forward Verne Reynold scored to bring the score to 22-17. The momentum had switched sides.

But then either Litchfield and Lemmon on the bench or the players themselves in a sideline huddle devised a spur of the moment out-of-bounds play: While Stan Buckingham pretended to throw the ball in to either Wallace or Kessler, brother Frank sneaked under the basket, took the inbounds pass, and scored. The play worked so well that it seemed to demoralize Lincoln, Bellfountain went back on the attack and, led by Kessler's 13 points and Stan's 9, went on to win 35-21.

For the game, Bellfountain's almost impenetrable defense committed just four personal fouls, forced Lincoln into making only 9 of 64 shots from the field, and held star guard Lee Sitton scoreless, while its offense made 10 of 35 shots from the field and 15 of 17 from the free throw line—including Kessler's 9-9 free throw shooting. But statistics aside, the fact was that tiny Bellfountain had done what had been thought to be impossible, and the team's supporters went wild.

The pandemonium in the gym was deafening, and the cheers of approval ricocheted across the state. Newspaper headlines blazed the news about the small country school that had toppled the largest schools in the state while articles detailed how the Giant Killers had walked away with most of the tournament's awards and honors: the B League state trophy, the A League state trophy, the Individual Sportsmanship trophy to Richard Kessler, first team All State A honors for Kessler and Harry Wallace, second team All State A honors for Stanley Buckingham, and All State B honors for Kessler, Wallace, Buckingham, and Clifford Larkin.

In summing up the abilities of the two Bellfountain basketball players who made the All-State first team, the *Eugene Register-Guard* called Kessler a "faultless ball handler" and Wallace the "spark plug of his team" as well as the "best dribbler in the tournament." In fact, Kessler's selection required that he beat out Astoria's 6-foot 4-inch Earl Sandness, who had broken the tournament's individual scoring record with 64 points.

Richard Kessler

In addition, Wallace was the only guard on the All-State A team, a local newspaper said, "to have been chosen unanimously by all of the 26 coaches, newspapermen, and tournament officials who participated in the selection."

Harry Wallace

Yet in spite of the honors heaped upon Kessler and Wallace, it was obvious that the victory belonged to the entire team, as well as to the community who had raised this team of Giant Killers.

A Season to Remember

After the tournament came the celebrations and banquets at Corvallis, Monroe, Bellfountain, and Eugene, where mayors gave the keys to their cities to the young Bellfountain coach and his basketball stars, and statewide dignitaries spoke in their honor, one of them comparing the team's display of sportsmanship both on and off the court to the chivalry shown by knights in the Middle Ages. And like some legendary knights, the Bells had also vanquished giants.

With their achievement cemented in history, four members of the team—Harrison Wallace, Richard Kessler, Stanley Buckingham, and Frank Buckingham—prepared to graduate in June. In his salutatory address that Harry wrote for graduation, he gave full credit for the championship to the players' parents because of the high morals and values taught to them at home.

Before graduation, Bellfountain students put together a yearbook for the first time in the school's history. It was made, one inscription

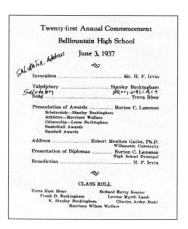

said, "in Honor of the Bellfountain High School Basketball team." That yearbook, however, would be both the first and the last ever printed for the school because a year after its historic basketball championship, Bellfountain consolidated with nearby Monroe High School.

Bellfountain students pose in front of their school for the 1937 yearbook

In the spring of 1937, The Oregon Statesman referred to Bellfountain as "that wide place in the road," a country village that historically was scantily populated and relatively insignificant. But all that changed when eight young men and two special coaches overcame overwhelming odds to win a state basketball championship by assuming the role of Giant Killers.

Appendix
What Happened to the Giant Killers

Frank Buckingham (starting guard, senior, graduated 1937). After graduating from Bellfountain High School in 1937, Frank served in the U.S. Air Force for four years. Then he and his wife Loraine took advantage of a government program for veterans and homesteaded in Pasco, Washington. Here he farmed and raised cattle for most of his life. In the 1937 High School year book Frank was named as the most improved player on the championship team. He died of a heart attack in 1997.

Stanley Buckingham (starting forward, senior, graduated 1937). Of the five starters on the championship team, Stanley was the only one to complete college, earning a B.S. degree from Oregon State College (now Oregon State University) in Corvallis. He then joined the service and spent four years in

the infantry. Like his brother Frank, Stan took advantage of the government homestead offer, and he and his wife Eileen raised potatoes and other crops near Tulelake, California. He farmed this land until he was killed in a 1990 automobile accident in Indio, California.

Alvah Hinton (starting guard on the 1935-36 team that placed third at state, graduated 1936). Following his graduation from Bellfountain, Alvah worked in the logging industry until 1937, when he joined Richard Kessler in

Alvah Hinton
2002

attending Oregon State College. At the end of that school year, Alvah went back to work in the logging industry until 1944, when he joined the Merchant Marines and served until 1946. He then worked for the Clemen's Lumber Company until he retired at the age of 62. After more than 30 years of marriage, Alvah's wife Louisa died in 1987, and today he lives in Corvallis, Oregon.

Lynn Hinton (substitute, sophomore, graduated 1939). After graduating from Monroe High School, into which Bellfountain had been consolidated, Lynn joined the navy and served until the end of World War II. In October of 1945 he married Suzan, who was from Massachusetts, and together they raised two children, Larry and Rita. In 1946 he went to work for the Bell Telephone Company in Portland as an installer, and retired from the company in 1979. "It was the most outstanding thing I was ever associated with," Lynn said of his involvement with the Giant Killers, "even though I was a spectator." He died March 21, 2002 of cancer.

Lynn Hinton
1937

Norman Humphrey (substitute, sophomore, graduated 1939). Following his graduation from Monroe and his time spent in the service, Norman married Mary Jane Key, who had been a classmate at Bellfountain, and together they raised a large family. Norman spent most of his life in the Bellfountain area logging, farming, or driving machinery. He died in 1993 of a heart attack.

Norman Humphrey
1937

Richard Kessler (starting center, senior, graduated 1937). Even though he was recruited by Oregon State College as a basketball player, Richard left college after his first year. He and his wife Audrey had two children, a daughter Anne and a son Richard, who died of cancer in 1974 at the age of 17. For most of his life Richard worked in the heavy construction industry around the Corvallis area for various builders and lumber companies as well as for himself. After retirement he became involved in golf and bowling. The Bellfountain yearbook emphasized the fact that Richard "never sacrificed his team play for his individual honors." This was probably one of the reasons he won the coveted Sportsmanship Trophy at the 1937 state championships. He died December 7, 1996 at Heart of the Valley Nursing Home at the age of 78.

John Key (substitute, sophomore, graduated 1939). After graduating from Monroe, John attended Oregon College of Education in Monmouth, where he married college classmate and Bellfountain graduate Louise Davis (a former girl friend of Richard Kessler). They had one daughter. John was killed at Okinawa in World War II.

John Key
1937

Clifford Larkin (starting forward, junior, graduated 1938). During a basketball game in his senior year of 1938, Clifford broke his leg and was unable to complete the season. Following his graduation from Bellfountain he worked in the logging industry, then went into the service, where he served during World War II as a tank commander in northern Africa. He spent two years in a German prison camp after his tank was destroyed on the battlefield. After the war Cliff married Louise Davis Key, widow of John Key (see above). Together they raised a boy and two girls. According to Cliff, he "farmed, drove a truck, worked for Oregon State University, and joined the sheriff's posse and cared for their horses." One of Cliff's most vivid memories of his Giant Killers experience was the way in which the famed squad brought the ball down the court from the defensive to the offensive end. "We would pass the ball so efficiently," he says, "that it would never touch the floor." Clifford has Parkinson's disease and resides in a care facility in Corvallis, Oregon.

Burton C. Lemmon (Bellfountain coach, 1936-37) After the championship season, Bill Lemmon left Bellfountain for a coaching job at Eatonville, Washington, where he coached basketball for three years. He then moved on to Clover Park High School and then to Stadium High School, his alma mater, in Tacoma, where he spent 12 years coaching. "I kept hoping I'd find another Bellfountain team, and I never did," he said some 40 years after the championship season. "Bellfountain ranks at the top in my educational and sports experiences." He died August 11, 1999 at the age of 87.

George Kenneth Litchfield (Bellfountain coach, 1929-1936). After leaving Bellfountain in 1936, Kenneth served one year as Shedd's superintendent of schools, then moved his family to Toledo, Oregon, where he practiced law with his uncle, George McCluskey. Three years later, in 1940, Ken moved to Newport and set up his own law practice. Over the next 40 years his contributions to the community were so extensive that the museum at Newport contains a replica of his office. He and Frances had five children—Carol, Donald, Ralph, Richard, and Ruth. Ken retired from his law practice in 1990 at the age of 84. Throughout his life, Coach Litchfield kept in contact with the Bellfountain community as well as with the members of its championship team. "Litchfield would say in later years," his obituary noted, "that [Bellfountain's state basketball championship] was perhaps his most gratifying personal achievement." He died May 5, 2000 at the age of 93.

Harry and Treva Wallace
2002

Harrison Wallace (starting guard, senior, graduated 1937). Oregon State College offered Harry a basketball scholarship, but he didn't accept it. Instead, after graduation he eloped with Treva Bloor, his childhood sweetheart, and went to work first for Wes Miller Lumber Company as a "whistle punk" and then for I. P. Lumber Company. In 1943-1944 Harry served in the service. After his discharge he spent the rest of his working life as a contract logger. He and Treva had three children: twins Billy Allen and Mary Ellen, and later Janene. Billy was killed in a tragic accident when he fell while climbing a tree in front of the Bellfountain grade school. Harry and Treva, who have been married for more than 65 years, live in Corvallis, Oregon.

Bellfountain School and its gym were purchased by the Bellfountain Community Church in November of 2000. The church rents the school to Bellfountain Cornerstone Christian School. In the main hallway of the elementary school is a trophy case containing the basketball team's trophies from the 1935, 1936, and 1937 seasons. The church is in charge of restoring and caring for them. Both the school and its gym are listed on the Benton County Register of Historic Places.

Bellfountain School
2002

The Bellfountain Giant Killers after their state championship in 1937

Top (from left): Bill Lemmon, Stanley Buckingham, Harry Wallace, Richard Kessler, Frank Buckingham, Clifford Larkin, Norman Humphrey

Kneeling: Lynn Hinton, John Key

The Bellfountain Giant Killers at their 40th reunion in 1977

Top (from left): Bill Lemmon, Stanley Buckingham, Harry Wallace, Richard Kessler, Frank Buckingham, Clifford Larkin, Norman Humphrey

Kneeling: Lynn Hinton.

Missing: John Key, who was killed in action during World War II

About the Author

Even though he was born in California and earned a degree in history from San Diego State College, Joe Blakely has lived most of his life in Eugene, Oregon, where his various careers have included selling and appraising real estate, repairing and refinishing furniture, and working with the Office of Public Safety at the University of Oregon before his retirement in 1999. But it was a chance encounter that made him an author. It began while he was researching and photographing the historic Hull-Oakes Lumber Mill south of Corvallis.

Joe Blakely

Photograph by Saundra Miles

"Every time I drove to that lumber mill," he says, "I would pass the Bellfountain school. Then one day I read Bob Welch's 'Little Known Facts about Oregon' column in the Eugene *Register-Guard*, and one of those facts described tiny Bellfountain High School's 1937 state champion basketball team known as the Giant Killers." His interest piqued, Joe decided to write about the team. He soon discovered, however, that the story involved much more than just basketball.

"My research uncovered a period of time almost pristine in its gentle beauty," he says. "This was a time when basketball was played with finesse and when sportsmanship was praised and admired. It was also a time when the smallest school in Oregon could challenge the largest. Some of the people involved in this story are among the humblest yet most inspirational people I have ever met."

Books unique to the Northwest

E stablished in 1999, Bear Creek Press of Wallowa, Oregon, specializes in publishing books unique to the Pacific Northwest, especially those that capture the life or preserve the history of the region.

For more information or a free catalog:

Bear Creek Press
814 Couch Avenue • Wallowa, Oregon 97885
541-886-9020 • bearcreekpress@eoni.com
www.bearcreekpress.com

Bear Creek Press gives one-day service on all orders
and an unconditional guarantee on all books.